FIRST AID FOR GRIEF

A GUIDE TO STEER YOU THROUGH LOSS

BY

JO NAUGHTON

Grosvenor House
Publishing Limited

This book is published by
Grosvenor House Publishing Ltd
Link House
140 The Broadway, Tolworth, Surrey, KT6 7HT.
www.grosvenorhousepublishing.co.uk

A CIP record for this book
is available from the British Library

Paperback ISBN 978-1-83615-478-5
eBook ISBN 978-1-83615-479-2

Some names and details have been changed to protect the
identity of the people whose stories are included in this book.
Bible references are from the New King James
Version unless otherwise stated. The Message and TPT
are also used to help reveal the heart of certain passages.

This book is dedicated to those who sat with us: Larissa, Clare, Scott, Eamon, Jennifer, Temi & Mary, Kelly & Remi.

ACKNOWLEDGMENTS

Thank you, Paolo; you showed me how to continue hoping when my heart was broken. You took the lead, and I followed.

Jane Oundjian, you taught me timeless truths that carried me through. I will always be grateful for your wisdom and kindness.

CONTENTS

Chapter 1

I AM SO SORRY

When someone you love passes away, the pain can be almost unbearable. I don't know what you are experiencing right now, but I know that at times, it can feel overwhelming. The weight of grief could be pressing heavily upon your chest, and the sorrow could seem unending. You may have an uncomfortable lump that refuses to leave the back of your throat. Perhaps you feel like you're drowning in sadness. Please know that you are not alone. The Holy Spirit is by your side right now, and He will stay with you throughout this season. Psalms 34:18 (NLT) says, "The LORD is close to the brokenhearted; He rescues those whose spirits are crushed." He is by your side because He cares. He will not leave you, even for a moment.

Our little girl was running around a shopping mall on a Monday. Naomi became very ill that Tuesday and was gone by 8 am on Wednesday morning. When the utter disbelief faded, I plunged into terrible grief. Because she was our only child when she died, my husband and I also lost our role as parents. I was devastated. If you had told me in the weeks after she passed away that my shattered heart would be made new, I would have told you that you were sorely mistaken. But God did what I thought was not possible. He led me on a precious journey to restoration, and He also mended my husband's broken heart. Since then, I have lost other family members, and although the route to recovery was different with each bereavement, He has healed me every time a loved one has passed away.

My journey has not only given me immense compassion for those who are grieving, but also a deep longing to see each one experience lasting restoration. Down through the years, God has given my husband and me the privilege of ministering to countless men and women who have been plunged into grief. We have watched the Lord bring relief and healing to many precious people. Tragedies that they thought would mark them forever became testimonies of our Heavenly Father's power to restore. What God did for me, my husband, and many others, He is able to do for you.

A Way Through

You might be in the midst of grief right now, or you may be reading this book because you are seeking to support a friend or church member. Maybe you have a heart for those who are grieving and want to learn how to help. If you are reading out of a love for people, I believe that the Lord will give you insights and understanding to help you accompany others during times of loss. You will gain tools so that you can assist them on a journey towards restoration. Thank you for caring so much that you are investing in equipping yourself.

If you have lost someone dear, this book will help you through the first few seasons of life after the death of your loved one. Although I encourage you to read it from start to finish, you may also find it helpful to jump to relevant chapters to find help when you need it the most. For example, before returning to familiar places or before a first birthday or holiday without them, please go to my chapter "Facing Your Firsts". If you have a difficult experience with someone who doesn't respond well to your pain, go straight to "People". By God's grace, you will find help to navigate the road ahead.

A Journey To Recovery

It may feel as though you will never recover, but I want you to know that you can come out of this sorrow. Sometimes when someone we love passes away, it can feel as though something on the inside of us died with them. Psalms 30:2–3 says, "O LORD my God, I cried out to You, and You healed me. O LORD, You brought my soul up from the grave…" If that's how you feel, your Heavenly Father wants to bring you up from that place and restore you back to life. It will probably be a journey, but there is a way out of this sad wilderness.

I have witnessed women who lost their husbands in their prime restored to joy. Fathers and mothers whose children passed away in traumatic circumstances have rebuilt rewarding lives. Men and women who lost friends, siblings, parents, and other loved ones have come out the other side restored. The enemy may try to tell you that you will never recover, but let me repeat an earlier sentiment: what the Lord has done for me, my husband, and many others, He would love to do for you too.

When Healing Flowed

Kate's son Ben died when he was just eight years old following a long battle with sickness. After he passed away, the Lord graciously gave this precious mom a vision of Ben in heaven, which brought her a great deal of comfort. However, when Ben died, Kate felt like a part of her died too. She just wanted to be in heaven with her son, despite having a family that needed her here on earth. Two years after Kate's loss, she attended one of our conferences called "Healed for Life".

"As I listened to Jo talk about the death of her daughter, I could not stop crying. Overwhelming grief welled up from the depths of my soul." Kate continued, "As I wept, the Lord did a supernatural work inside me. He restored the shattered places in my soul and healed my broken heart. God lifted a heavy weight of disappointment and oppression. I remember going to bed feeling an excitement and joy that I had never before experienced. Before leaving that conference, the Lord showed me that just as an onion has layers, so my restoration would go deeper and deeper, one layer at a time."

After that first encounter, Kate continued attending our events and went on a wonderful healing journey. She explained, "Now when I look back, I no longer feel any grief. Instead, I have an immense sense of joy and gratitude. I am part of the Whole Heart Ministries team and have the privilege of helping others on their way to total restoration." What God did for Kate, He can do for you too.

You're Not Alone

Many of our Bible heroes experienced the terrible pain of loss. They suffered the agony of bereavement but came out the other side. Let me share a few examples. Two of Judah's sons died, and yet his tribe went on to carry the seed of Christ, our Messiah. Both of Esther's parents died when she was just a little girl; nevertheless, she became the queen of a foreign country. Mephibosheth lost both his dad, his grandfather, and the ability to walk, in one terrible day, but was taken in by King David to live at the palace. Ruth's husband tragically died while she was young, but she went on to experience joy again and was named in the lineage of Jesus. You may be weighed down with great pain right now, but I want you to know there is a way to be free from this sadness.

Psalms 147:3 (TPT) says, "He heals the wounds of every shattered heart." It is not just that I have faith in this verse; I know it to be true. None of us has all the answers to hard questions, but I can tell you this: your Heavenly Father desires to restore your soul. After our daughter died, I wanted her back, so I wanted a resurrection. But when that short-lived dream was dashed, I decided—reluctantly at first— that I would seek a different miracle: the healing of my heart. Every time I brought a broken piece of my soul to the Lord, He lovingly restored me. I encourage you to open your heart to Jesus and start the process of surrendering your pain to Him.

One of the reasons that God sent Jesus to the earth was to heal the brokenhearted and comfort those who have been bereaved. Speaking of Christ, the Bible says in Isaiah 61:1b: "...He has sent Me to heal the brokenhearted..." Again, in Isaiah 61:2–3, it says that Jesus came: "... To comfort all who mourn, to console those who mourn in Zion..." That's how much the Lord cares about relieving your sorrow.

Each chapter in this book provides practical tools that will help you to deal with the difficulties of bereavement. I have kept each section short in case you are finding it hard to concentrate. If you would like additional resources, my husband and I have another book that is dedicated to healing after loss called *How To Rise From The Ashes Of Tragedy*. Also, my books, *Let's Talk About Trauma* and *My Pretend Friend*, will bring restoration. As we begin this journey together, I would love to lead you in prayer:

Heavenly Father,

I come to You today with a broken heart. This hurts terribly. I loved (insert the name of your loved one) so much and I miss them more than I can explain. However, I want to find my way out of this pain and towards restoration. Lord, You know the things that have been hardest for me and You know the challenges ahead of me, so I ask You to help me to walk through this difficult season. I ask You to give me the tools that will help me to come out the other side.

Even though it feels very painful, I open my heart to You, Lord.

Help me on this journey, I pray.

In Jesus' name, Amen.

Chapter 2

SHOCK & DISBELIEF

The finality of separation can seem both unfathomable and brutal. Even when you know that someone is going to pass away, the realization that they have actually gone can be shocking. Perhaps the fact that you will not see your loved one again this side of eternity feels surreal. They were with you one moment, then with a final breath, they were gone. Their warmth, their touch, their smile, their very presence in your life somehow evaporated. Please don't underestimate the impact of shock. It can disrupt your sleep, steal your appetite, interfere with your digestion, and shake you to the core.

In the early days after losing someone you love, you may momentarily forget that they have gone. You could reach for the phone to call them, you may open your mouth to ask them a question, or you might be in your own world and then suddenly remember your new reality. It might feel as though you are repeatedly being bombarded with the distress of their death as though it just happened. Any time this happens, please don't internalize the pain. Turn to the Lord and tell Him exactly what you are feeling in that moment; talk to Him about every detail, knowing that He cares. If it's shock, tell Him. If it's pain, explain what you're experiencing. If it's anger, speak to Him about that. Your Wonderful Counselor is by your side and ready to hear, and then heal, the distress of your soul.

When our daughter died, life as I knew it came to an abrupt end. I was dazed for days as the reality of our tragedy gradually unfolded in my heart. The night after Naomi passed away, I fell asleep at the dining table in a friend's home halfway through my dinner. My fork, which slipped out of my hand and fell on the table, woke me. This bizarre moment sums up my state during the first few days after our daughter's departure. Mornings were awful for me. I would usually forget what had happened for the first few seconds after waking. My head would turn to check our toddler monitor in the corner of the room. The moment I saw that it was turned off, I would remember that my precious daughter was gone.

Shaken By Shock

"A horrible and shocking thing has happened..." (Jeremiah 5:30, NLT). Let me repeat what I said at the start of this chapter, please don't underestimate the impact of shock. It comes like a punch in the guts and can cause even strong people to be shaken to the core. Some of the Bible's greatest leaders experienced its force: "… I, Daniel, was in shock. I was like a man who had seen a ghost…" (Daniel 7:28, MSG). Your chest might have become tight, or your mind foggy. Your stomach could have crunched, or you may have been faint. You could have felt disconnected from what happened, like you were watching a movie of events unfolding. Perhaps you experienced intense anger or maybe everything inside of you wanted to run from the situation.

If you have been winded by your loss, I want you to know that the Lord desires to reach into any chaos raging inside your soul and bring His calming comfort. Sometimes you need to shout or cry aloud in order to release the depths of distress. You can talk to God about your disbelief and any alarm. He is not faint-hearted; He can handle your anguish and will remain by your side through any times of anger or dismay. One caution: in a desire to help or protect others, please don't bury your own pain. Share your heart with your Heavenly Father in prayer; tell Him how you are feeling; anguish is always better out than hidden inside your soul.

A False Sense Of Security

The loss of a loved one is almost always heartbreaking. But when it is a bolt out of the blue, the impact can be even more ferocious. Perhaps you were at ease, certain that everything would work out, and then suddenly, they went rapidly downhill. 1 Thessalonians 5:3 says, "…they say, 'Peace and safety!'" then sudden destruction comes upon them, as labor pains upon a pregnant woman…" Although I had attended classes and heard stories about giving birth, I was not really prepared for the agony or the intensity. Like many women, I was overwhelmed. The verse above explains that tragedy is similar in its ability to overwhelm, but without a precious child to soothe your soul.

Your loved one may have died in a terrible accident or been the victim of a crime. They could have suddenly been hit with sickness or suffered an unexpected heart attack or hemorrhage. When this happens, there is not even a moment to prepare for such a tragedy. It can feel like being hit by a truck on the highway. As part of your journey to restoration, you will need to deal with the serious blow as well as the inevitable grief. Please don't bury the horror or turn away from the brutality of the shock. I know it's hard, but please bring this pain to the Lord in prayer; share exactly how you're feeling with God.

Traumatic Memories

You may have been traumatized by your memories of the final hours before your loved one died. Job 21:6 (MSG) says, "When I look back, I go into shock, my body is racked with spasms." If reminders of what they went through cause distress, the Lord wants to relieve that pain. Any recollection that brings dread is a memory that God wants to heal. In the first few weeks after our daughter died, I was

11

tormented by memories of the final 24 hours of her life. In my mind's eye, I would see her curled up in a fetal position in the bed beside me. Then I would picture her little frame hooked up to far too many medical machines. I would see myself pacing up and down the corridor while they tried to revive her after she went into cardiac arrest. Those memories were filled with dread, so I did everything I could to avoid them. But while I avoided them, they tormented me. When I made the decision to talk to the Lord about those experiences and share my distress with Him, the trauma was diffused and I began the journey to healing.

Perhaps for you, as the shock has begun to evaporate, it has left behind a deadness on the inside. You may be living under a cloud of bewilderment. You may feel like the life has been sucked out of you and you are just going through the motions. When you have dealt with the shock in prayer, you will feel more able to face the rest of your pain and enter a season of healing. I would love to lead you in prayer to deal with shock.

Heavenly Father,

The shock of (insert your loved one's name) passing has left me feeling winded and bewildered. I cannot quite believe that I will not see them again this side of eternity. I am struggling to come to terms with what has happened. My loved one was here one moment and gone the next. It feels unreal and cruel. I don't want to remain shaken, Lord. I don't want nervousness or distress to dominate my thoughts and emotions. I don't want any dread buried in my soul. (Now tell the Lord what shocked you the most. Share your disbelief or distress with God. Describe your feelings in as much detail as possible. If you need to shout, or cry aloud, please don't hold back.) Lord, I give You my shock, I give You my feelings of disbelief, I give You any horror. I ask You to calm my heart with Your wonderful healing love.

There are certain memories that shook me, Lord, even looking back at them feels traumatic. (Now tell the Lord about any distressing memories, share what happened and how you felt in that moment. Tell Him why it was so painful. Talk to Him in as much detail as possible.) I ask You to heal my heart, Lord. I bring every distressing memory to You, Lord. I bring You my fears and sorrow. I bring You my anguish and sadness. Thank You for leading me on a journey to relief and restoration. I ask You to fill my heart with Your love; I need to feel Your closeness, Lord. I receive Your peace into the depths of my being today. I draw close to You in this painful time, Heavenly Father. Thank You for staying close to me.

In Jesus' name I pray,

Amen.

Chapter 3

PAIN RELIEF

The ache of grief can be hard to bear. Proverbs 15:13 (MSG) says: "A sad heart makes it hard to get through the day." Very often, the pain comes in waves that can feel overwhelming. You may be okay, then a reminder of your loved one causes an avalanche of sorrow. The sheer depths of sadness can drain your strength so that you feel like you're running on empty. You may be getting on with life and work, but deep inside, you know that you're just going through the motions. Perhaps you feel a constant ache inside.

Proverbs 15:13 in the NKJV says, "By sorrow of the heart the spirit is broken." In Hebrew, the word translated in this verse as "spirit" literally means "breath of life". So this verse is saying that lasting sadness can extinguish your zeal; it can choke the very life out of you. You can end up feeling parched and detached. It can also numb your relationship with the Lord because you and I commune with Him from our hearts—the very place that sorrow is situated. You may feel like you're in a spiritual wilderness as well as being in emotional pain. In order to come through this season, you need to know His presence. As you pour out your pain in prayer, the weight of grief will begin to lessen. But there is another precious benefit: you will experience the life of the Lord flowing into your heart again.

Unhelpful Emotional Habits

Maybe you have learned in the past to swallow your pain, toughen up, then carry on. You may have been raised in a culture that associates weeping with weakness. Perhaps, while you were growing up, you heard sentiments such as, "Dry up", "Don't be such a sissy", or "Get over it". As a result, you've conditioned yourself to bury your emotions. But pushing down pain does not make it go away; it causes it to sink to the bottom of your soul. The Bible teaches us a very different way to deal with pain. Ecclesiastes 11:10 says, "…remove sorrow from your heart…"

I have ministered healing to many people who had buried their grief at the time of their loss. Two decades after Tom's mother died, he attended one of our meetings. Tom's mom was also his friend and the kindest person he had ever met. Her sudden death was a massive shock. As a caring person himself, the moment tragedy struck, Tom stepped into a support role, helping everyone else to heal. His own pain somehow got ignored and buried deep inside. Any mention of his mom would cause Tom sadness, even years after she died. When I shared about God's power to heal all grief, Tom broke down and wept as deep wells of pain suddenly erupted. He howled as the Lord healed his heart. After an hour of weeping and healing, peace descended. Tom never felt any sorrow again. You don't need to wait years to experience genuine relief, but if you have buried your pain, God is still able to restore your soul. Whether it's old wounds or recent sorrow, please share your pain with the Lord any time you're sad.

You may hide how much you're hurting. Perhaps you wear a smile, tell people that you are fine, and try not to think about your loss. Unfortunately, ignoring sorrow does not stop it causing harm. Proverbs 14:13 (NLT) says, "Laughter can conceal a heavy heart, but when the laughter ends, the grief remains." The Lord doesn't want you to cover up your sadness; He wants to take it away. After our daughter died, I learned a vital lesson: pain is better out than in. Wherever I was, if sorrow built up, I would find a way to let it out. Occasionally, I would cry on my train journey home from work. If I was with friends, I told them how I was feeling, and at work, I would find a private place to deal with my grief.

You may struggle to share your difficulties with friends or family. Perhaps you consider deep emotions to be very private. The truth is that we need one another, especially in times of suffering. There is a reason why Psalms 68:6a (NIV) says, "God sets the lonely in families…" Our Heavenly

Father intended for us to have meaningful and loving relationships. There may be a word of wisdom or a life-giving prayer in the mouth of a brother or sister at church. It is helpful to share your journey with a couple of trusted friends. Talking is healthy and will help you come out the other side. However, what is most important is that you share your heart with the Lord. As you pour out your pain in prayer before your Heavenly Father, He will bring lasting healing. Please don't keep your sorrow to yourself.

Start Today

Several years ago, my husband and I went through a big ministry disappointment. The night it all blew up, I lay awake in bed feeling heartbroken. The Lord brought Proverbs 18:14 to my remembrance: "Who can bear a broken spirit?" I realized that something deep down had broken and that I couldn't bear the pain. Getting out of bed, I knelt down and called out to God: "I can't carry on while my heart is so sore." I told Him how much I was hurting, and cried in His presence. Talking to the Lord from my heart, I told Him what had upset me most. As I poured out my pain before Him, God tended to my wounds. I felt the sorrow lift and went back to bed, tired but relieved. I slept soundly and woke up the next morning at peace.

One of the reasons that the enemy tries to tempt us into internalizing our pain is that heartbreak wears us down. Proverbs 17:22 (NLT) says, "A broken spirit saps a person's strength." When you have lost someone you love, you need all the strength you can get, so getting your pain out is vital. Genesis 35:3 says, "Let us arise and go up to Bethel and I will make an altar there to God who answered me in the day of my distress and has been with me in the way." There are two precious truths contained in this verse. If you will go to your Heavenly Father in the midst of grief, He will meet with you and relieve your sorrow, but it doesn't stop there; as you turn to Him every time you are hurting, He will journey with you until your heart is made whole.

Perhaps you have never asked the Lord to heal your heart before. I suggest you start today. Any time pain surfaces, shut your eyes and tell the Lord how you feel that moment. If you are missing your loved one, tell Jesus: "I miss them, Lord. I miss their smile, their advice, their love. It hurts, Lord!" Turn your pain into a prayer. It does not matter whether it is a little reminder of your loved one or agony in the middle of the night. Share your heart with God and ask Him to take your pain away.

Maybe you already seek God's healing occasionally, when you are at church or in a prayer meeting. There is no reason to wait. Bring every source of sadness to Him whenever it surfaces. The Bible tells us to become like children in our relationship with Jesus (see Matthew 18:3). Children know how to let out pain. If something upset my daughter when she was young, she would run straight into my arms and tell me what had happened. She would recount who did what and how it made her feel. Within a few moments, her tears would dry up as she would enjoy a reassuring cuddle. We need to learn to come to our Heavenly Father as a child. After all, as 2 Corinthians 1:3 says, He is "…the Father of mercies and God of all comfort."

Your Wonderful Counselor

One of the names given to Jesus is "Wonderful Counselor" (see Isaiah 9:6). Counseling is only effective when a client shares from their heart. If people can be helped by an earthly counselor, imagine the power of sharing your heart with your heavenly Counselor, Jesus Christ. King David understood this principle more than most. He shared the depths of his pain with the Lord. After his best friend died, he cried aloud in 2 Samuel 1:25–27 (NLT): "Oh, how mighty heroes have fallen in battle! Jonathan lies dead on the hills. How I weep for you, my brother Jonathan! Oh, how much I loved you! And your love for me was deep, deeper than the love of women! Oh, how the mighty heroes have fallen! Stripped of their weapons, they lie dead." David (hailed in Scripture as 'the man after God's own heart') turned his pain into a prayer and released his anguish in God's presence.

You and I have been designed with a divine connection between our hearts and our mouths. Luke 6:45b says, "… out of the abundance of the heart his mouth speaks." Just as unscrewing the lid of a bottle enables you to pour out a drink, so talking opens the door of your heart, giving buried pain a way out. Speaking to someone you trust about your experiences gives trapped distress a voice and a means of release. Sharing your pain with the Lord goes much further. It is not just helpful; it makes the way for an exchange. You give your angst and sadness to Him. In return, He pours out His healing love into your heart. This leads to lasting relief.

When you are hurting, please tell the Lord what is going on inside. You don't need to sanitize your thoughts; you can share your most private and uncomfortable feelings with Him. He will not be shocked or offended. Scripture says, "Trust in Him at all times, you people; pour out your heart before Him; God is a refuge for us." (Psalm 62:8) Sharing your heart with God releases pent-up pain and tension. It also builds trust in your relationship with Him. While the Lord listens to you as you share your heart, you will experience the warmth and closeness of His wonderful love.

After sharing your sorrow with God in prayer, you will feel genuine relief. Each time you talk to Him, another precious piece of your shattered soul will be restored. Luke 6:21b (TPT) provides us with a wonderful promise: "…weep with complete brokenness, for you will laugh with unrestrained joy." I'm sure it will be a journey of healing encounters in His presence, but the season of pain will come to an end. Let's pray.

Heavenly Father,

I don't want to keep all this sadness trapped inside any longer. The pain of losing (insert the name of your loved one) feels like it's too much for me. I miss them so much, Lord. (Now tell the Lord what you miss the most; share your heart in as much detail as possible.) Certain memories hurt so much, Lord. (Now tell Jesus which memories cause you most pain. Describe each recollection, one by one. You may struggle most with trauma or untold suffering leading to their death. You could keep remembering a horrible conversation. It could be something else. Tell the Lord what happened—even the little details. Imagine that you are back in that place. Speak to Him about how it all made you feel. Open your heart to Him and tell Him about every hurt or question that you are holding inside.) I invite You, Lord, into every distressing memory. Take this pain away, Jesus; remove this sorrow from my heart. I give it to You today.

Your Word says that You heal the brokenhearted. I ask for Your healing love to flow into my soul right now. Come and restore me, Lord. I open my heart to You and I invite You to fill every corner of my soul with Your love. Jesus, You are a miracle-worker and I put my trust in Your ability to make me whole. I give You my heart.

In Jesus' name I pray,

Amen.

Chapter 4

FACING YOUR FIRSTS

Punching a street name and zip code into my GPS, I headed to a meeting with one of our church leaders. About five minutes before arriving, I looked up at a signpost that was announcing the destination: I was back in the town where my daughter had died just two months earlier. My head started spinning as indistinguishable emotion erupted inside. Pulling off the road, I parked up, stunned. What made it so difficult was the fact that I was not ready to be back in that town, just minutes from that hospital. I was still full of raw and unrehearsed memories. I want to help you to be more prepared than I was that day—at least for some of your inevitable firsts.

After you lose someone, going back to the places that you used to visit together can be very difficult. You may have attended church with your loved one or eaten at certain restaurants. The two of you could have shopped at particular stores or local malls. Then there are the friends and family that you may have visited together. Perhaps you endured a string of distressing visits to a certain hospital. Going back to these places or seeing certain faces for the first time can be very distressing. However, if you anticipate these moments, they will be less difficult. Let me explain.

Go There In Prayer

The Lord has given me a tool that will help you to prepare for foreseeable firsts. If you will adopt this approach, it will take some of the overwhelm out of these experiences. The principle can be summed up like this: go there in prayer before you go there in person. If a birthday is approaching or Christmas is coming, set aside some time in the presence of the Lord to pray through what you are about to go through. Imagine Christmas without your loved one. See the chair where they would have sat. Picture the day unfolding without them and tell the Lord how you feel. Don't hold back; release your sadness in His presence. Tell Him what you will miss the most and share any anxiety with God: "Pour out your heart like water before the face of the Lord" (Lamentations 2:19b). If you do that, the sting will be taken out of that experience in advance and you will be better prepared to face the day.

Proverbs 16:1 says, "The preparations of the heart belong to man, but the answer of the tongue is from the LORD." As you prepare your heart with the help of God, you will experience heaven's gracious answers. You will be able to focus on the fact that the Lord is right beside you instead of being overwhelmed by the absence of your loved one. I don't know how many times I have used this principle to help myself face an unpleasant experience on the horizon.

Which Firsts Do You Have To Face?

It is worth considering your firsts in advance. It is not just Christmas and birthdays, but a trip to the supermarket, worshipping in church, visiting family, and going on vacation. Think about your routines and the people or places that you used to visit together and will return to alone. By preparing, you will be able to alleviate some of the shock and pain. When we don't preempt a difficult situation, we can end up being overwhelmed or shaken. Philippians 4:6 (TPT) says, "Don't be pulled in different directions or worried about a thing. Be saturated in prayer throughout each day, offering your faith-filled requests before God with overflowing gratitude. Tell him every detail of your life."

Mario's little brother, Michael, died in tragic circumstances. Because the boys spent four years together in foster care, they had a very strong bond. Mario was protective of his younger brother, so when Michael was killed, Mario was distraught. He said it felt like he had been hit by a truck. Mario attended our Heart Academy Zoom course: "Life After The Death Of A Loved One". Week by week, his soul was restored. But it did not stop there. Mario learned how to prepare himself in advance of family reunions. Rather than avoiding anything that reminded him of his brother, he learned to go to each gathering in prayer, which enabled him to show up in person. Instead of becoming isolated, he was able to maintain family contact. By the end of the course, Mario no longer felt the unbearable pain that had weighed him down ever since his brother's untimely death.

Many men and women have used this tool to help them drive to particular towns again, eat at certain restaurants, or meet up with old friends. If you know you're going somewhere that may stir pain, please prepare your heart ahead. We have all heard of flashbacks. Based on this approach, I coined the phrase, "flash-forward". It is intentionally looking ahead to inevitable events and talking to God about them before they happen. Certain difficulties are in our future, and instead of avoiding thinking about them, you and I can be ready. Ecclesiastes 1:9–10 says, "That which has been is what will be, that which is done is what will be done, and there is nothing new under the sun. Is there anything of which it may be said, 'See, this is new'? It has already been in ancient times before us."

Five years before Pete's father passed away, the family had an unexpected health scare. This made Pete realize that he was not ready for his father to die. He had heard me share this teaching, so created time to go into God's presence and share his fears about his father passing away. He looked at what was inevitable at some point in the future. He shed a few tears and felt the love of God fill his prayer closet. Peace filled Pete's heart and he never again feared his dad's death. When his father did die, Pete grieved, but he was not shocked and he was healed more quickly than he thought possible.

A Prayer To Help You Prepare For Your Firsts

You can come back to this prayer any time you are facing a first. Your first time with certain friends or family, your first time at particular events or places, first birthdays, first Christmases, and also the first anniversary of their death.

Heavenly Father,

I can hardly believe that I am about to approach this without _____ (insert the name of your loved one). I never wanted to be in this position and the thought of facing this without them is overwhelming. However, I want to take the sting out of the pain of this first, so I have decided to go there in prayer, first. Lord, I am about to (now tell the Lord which first you are about to experience without your loved one.) I ask for Your help to deal with some of the distress and anxiety ahead of time. (Now picture yourself there without your loved one. See that chair where they used to sit, or the part that they used to play.) Lord, this hurts. I love them and I miss them. (Now tell the Lord exactly how you feel; tell Him about your deepest emotions, share your sorrow, any anger, or anxiety with Him freely.)

I ask You to reach into the depths of my heart and pull out this pain. I will not cling on to the sorrow of facing this without them; I ask You to take this agony away. I give You my distress, I give You my angst, I give You my turmoil. Have it all, Lord. Instead, I ask You to pour Your precious healing love into the empty spaces of my soul. Fill me with Your peace. Thank You that I will not go to these places on my own. You will be by my side every step of the way; I will not be alone. Thank You for Your love; You are my ever-present help and my closest companion. You are my Rock and my Comforter.

In Jesus' name I pray,

Amen.

Chapter 5

PEOPLE

Sean was in the middle of a business deal when he had a massive heart attack. Never regaining consciousness, Sean was declared dead at the scene by paramedics. The shock to his wife, Deborah, was colossal. Sean and Deborah's children were young adults who now had families of their own, so after the funeral, they returned to their respective homes. Deborah was now alone in a huge, empty house filled only with memories. Although she knew friends and family wanted to help, Deborah felt utterly alone. The sadness and loneliness were overwhelming. Unable to handle the void she now felt, Deborah filled her life with activity. She joined clubs, accompanied family any time they went on vacation, met up with friends; in short, Deborah booked up virtually every spare moment of her week.

When The Crowds Leave

There is a temptation when pain is great to run away from your new reality. The rationale follows something like this: "If I don't think about it, I won't have to face it. If I distract myself from the grief, it will lose its grip on my heart." As I mentioned earlier in this book, ignoring emotional pain does not make it go away. Avoiding grief will not remove the sadness from your soul. You may manage to dull the ache temporarily, but the pain will just get buried inside. Proverbs 14:13 (NLT) says, "Laughter can conceal a heavy heart, but when the laughter ends, the grief remains." After many months of nonstop activity designed to distract her from her new reality, Deborah broke down. It was at this time that she began to deal with her hidden sorrow. It was only when she allowed herself time to grieve that she began to heal.

While getting out of the house and finding meaningful things to do is very healthy during seasons of loss, it is also vital that you come back home and allow yourself time to come to terms with your new circumstances. Too many distractions will only delay your healing journey and may even cause your grief to get buried deep inside. There is a balance to strike: too much solitude could lengthen your walk through the valley, but too little "alone time" can lead to unresolved pain sinking to the bottom of your soul.

Drawing Close To Friends Or Family

Let's look again at the Old Testament story of Naomi's life told in Ruth 1:1–5 (NLT): "... a man from Bethlehem in Judah left his home and went to live in the country of Moab, taking his wife and two sons with him. The man's name was Elimelech, and his wife was Naomi. Their two sons were Mahlon and Kilion… Then Elimelech died, and Naomi was left with her two sons... One married a woman named Orpah, and the other a woman named Ruth. But about ten years later, both Mahlon and Kilion died. This left Naomi alone, without her two sons or her husband."

Naomi lost the three loves of her life—her husband and her two sons—while she was living in a foreign country. Maybe the culture was unfamiliar, perhaps she didn't speak the language; it could be that they dealt differently with loss. With all her immediate family gone, Naomi felt entirely alone. When you are engulfed in grief, living in a strange place can add to the pain and strain. Being around people who don't know or understand you can make a difficult situation harder. Considering her newfound reality, Naomi decided to move back home to Bethlehem.

When you have suffered a big loss, it is important to build a support network. It's not always those you have known the longest who provide the most comfort. We are all different and each one has unique abilities. Ephesians 4:7 (NLT) explains, "… He has given each one of us a special gift through the generosity of Christ." Your oldest friends might not know what to say or how to help, but a recent acquaintance may step into the breach and become a pillar in your life. Again, it says in Ephesians 4:16

(NLT), "He makes the whole body fit together perfectly. As each part does its own special work, it helps the other parts grow, so that the whole body is healthy and growing and full of love." It could save you unnecessary pain if you don't expect too much from people, and instead choose to appreciate any kindness offered. You may be surprised at the support that comes from an unexpected place.

Who Is There?

If you don't yet have two or three people in your corner, prayerfully ask the Lord to provide. Ask Him to show you who might be able to stand with you in this season. We can't always wait for people to come to us; sometimes they don't know how to offer help and may worry that they are intruding. Asking gives friends permission to draw close and help.

Let's go back to the story of Naomi told in the book of Ruth. When she was bereaved, Naomi thought that she was completely alone. However, God had a very special young woman called Ruth waiting in the wings to become a close companion. There are times when we think that we have nothing or no one, but if we look hard enough, we will be able to see God's provision.

Having made the decision to move back home, it was time for Naomi to say goodbye to her two daughters-in-law. Following a painful farewell, one turned back to her family. But let's look at Naomi's conversation with her other daughter-in-law, Ruth: "Look," Naomi said to her, "your sister-in-law has gone back to her people and to her gods. You should do the same." But Ruth replied, "Don't ask me to leave you and turn back. Wherever you go, I will go; wherever you live, I will live. Your people will be my people, and your God will be my God." (Ruth 1:15–16, NLT) Ruth not only walked with Naomi through her season of grief; she also became a source of great joy in Naomi's future.

Awkward People

A few days after our two-year-old daughter died, my husband received a call from a well-respected pastor. Raising his voice to be heard above loud traffic noises, he bellowed from his car phone, "Sorry for your loss, Paul, but maybe it was for the best. She could have got to age fifteen, then been raped and murdered. You just never know." My husband was gobsmacked, to say the least.

Around the same time, we received a card quoting a verse taken from the story of Jesus raising Jairus's daughter from the dead: "Now all wept and mourned for her; but He said, 'Do not weep; she is not dead, but sleeping.'" (Luke 8:52). I'm so glad that Jairus's daughter was raised back to life, but our daughter's body was buried. Together with the verse above, this well-meaning woman also wrote, "Be strong, Paul and Jo." I remember wondering if this lady had any idea what we were going through.

Many good people don't know what to say or do when a friend or acquaintance loses someone they love. It can be tempting to make a mental note when they fall short, then hold them to account in imaginary conversations. Sometimes, we downgrade people in our friendship hierarchy because they were absent during our time of need. Unfortunately, holding a grudge against people who should have known better will only add to your grief. Ecclesiastes 7:21a provides such rich wisdom: "… do not take to heart everything people say…" Even when we are vulnerable, we can choose to brush off insensitivities or untimely remarks. We can remind ourselves that they probably don't understand because they have not walked in our shoes.

I encourage you to make a decision today to let people off when they let you down. It will help you more than you could know. Forgive their failings, release them from any wrongdoing, and choose to believe the best about the reasons for their shortfalls. If you continue loving those who prove to be inept in your time of suffering, it will save you from unnecessary additional pain. And you may save a friendship that is a great blessing to you in the future. Let's pray.

Heavenly Father,

The pain of losing (insert your loved one's name) has left me feeling bereft. I ask You to provide me with some people who will be able to walk with me through this difficult season. Please send me one or two people who can help me find my way to healing. I choose today to ask those around me for help. I won't assume that friends or family understand my needs. I will explain what they can do to help.

Some people have let me down. I thought they would be there for me, but they were missing in action. Others have said or done the wrong things and made matters worse. (Now tell the Lord how you have been let down. Explain to Him about things said or done that hurt you.) I choose today to let them off, Lord. They can't possibly understand because they have never walked in my shoes. I forgive them for failing me and falling short. I release them completely from wrongdoing. I ask You to bless them and help them. I lower my expectations of others, and instead, I will appreciate whatever kindnesses I am shown.

Thank You, Lord, that even when others walk away, You never leave me, You are always by my side. I ask You to fill my heart with Your love.

In Jesus' name I pray,

Amen.

Chapter 6

SHATTERED DREAMS

Knowing that I was going home to see my dad for the last time, I boarded a night flight to London. He had been given just days to live. After takeoff, I plugged in my headphones and pulled a blanket over my head as the reality of my dad's imminent departure hit me. First, I found myself thinking about how cold and closed my father was throughout my childhood. I never felt his embrace or heard him tell me that he loved me. Our only meaningful physical contact in those early years was harsh discipline. My first positive memory of my dad was him canceling a bank debt when I was 22 years old. I couldn't believe I had no happy memories with him before my twenties. For more than an hour, I cried as I grieved the father I never had. When my tears dried up, momentary calm filled my heart.

All of a sudden, I began to weep again. During my early twenties, my father stepped into my life as a mentor and friend. He taught me how to think strategically and arrange my ideas intelligently. It was my dad that coached me in writing and equipped me with the skills that have enabled me to author many books. The reality of losing my dad suddenly hit me like a ton of bricks. "I've only got one dad!" I cried aloud to the Lord (thank God airplanes are noisy), "I love him and I miss him already." Sobbing from the depths of my soul, I poured out deep grief in the presence of the Lord. I must have cried for a few hours. Soon after the sadness subsided, the captain announced our descent into London's Heathrow airport. I went straight from the airport to the hospital to spend four or five precious hours with my father before heading home.

Imperfect Love

I will never forget sitting at his bedside and telling my dad that I loved him. "I know you don't like emotionalism," I said with a half smile on my face, "But I want you to know that I love you." Because the Lord had healed many of the wrongs in our relationship the night before, now all I could see was what my dad got right. I continued, "I want you to know that you have been a good father. I still remember the day that you called me and secretly canceled my bank debt. It meant the world, dad."

The following day my brother called: "Jo, dad has died." As I reflected on this news, I realized in amazement that the Lord had done a deep work in my heart on that flight home. I could not feel any significant pain. I then understood a key to healing. The Holy Spirit led me to grieve the shortcomings of my relationship with my father before He brought me to the pain of my dad's death. One reason people sometimes get stuck in grief is that they don't deal with the sorrow of imperfect relationships or unfulfilled hopes.

Perhaps there were flaws in your relationship with your loved one. Maybe they behaved in ways that wounded you. It is not dishonorable to acknowledge the pain of an imperfect relationship. In fact, it is important and will aid your healing journey. You don't need to tell friends or family, but please talk to the Lord about any upsets, fights or shortcomings that bruised your heart. Psalms 51:6 says, "Behold, You desire truth in the inward parts, And in the hidden part You will make me to know wisdom." Tell the Lord the truth about any difficulties that wounded your soul. As you draw near to Him and share your heart, He will surround you with His perfect love.

Dealing With Disappointment

Proverbs 13:12 describes the impact of shattered dreams. It says, "Hope deferred makes the heart sick..." The word that is translated as "sick" in this verse also means "grieved, sore, and wounded". When someone you love dies, you feel the gaping hole of their absence, but you may also be grieving the loss of hopes or dreams of a future together.

Disappointment is a horrible mix of sadness and injustice. The sadness is the result of your deep desires being dashed. The person you love is gone. A sense of injustice arises because your expectations did not come to pass. What you longed to see happen did not happen. It can feel unfair, it can seem so wrong. In order to be free from the heavy weight of disappointment, you need to deal with both parts.

It is vital that you pour out the sorrow. Perhaps you had dreams of a future together or desires that never materialized. Maybe you struggle with uncomfortable memories of an imperfect relationship. If you have any sadness about "what never was", or "what never will be", God wants to heal your heart. If we don't face this unexpected, and often overlooked, source of grief, we can end up weighed down. In Psalm 119:28, King David told God how letdowns weighed heavily on his heart: "My soul melts from heaviness…" We can end up feeling disillusioned and heavyhearted if we leave such sadness buried inside.

The Issue with Injustice

The other part of disappointment is that horrible sense of injustice. Perhaps you were praying and believing but they died anyway. Maybe you had been standing on promises that didn't come to pass. You could feel terribly let down. After you have poured out the sorrow of disappointment, it is time to lay down the injustice. Many years ago I asked the Lord about this matter. "We all know what to do with sickness or unforgiveness," I told the Lord, "But what do we do with disappointment?" His response was immediate: "Lay it down as an offering."

King David refused to give God something that cost him nothing (see 2 Samuel 24:24). We have an opportunity when we feel let down. We can bring every sense of injustice to the Lord as an offering. Because it costs you a lot, it will mean a lot to God. I've done this many times now, and although it may be hard at first, the relief afterward is immense. Give the Lord every feeling of having been let down; offer Jesus your disappointment as a sacrifice. Bring it to Him and leave it at the foot of the Cross. Some burdens are just too heavy to carry, and this is one of them.

The enemy is always seeking to keep us away from the only One who can help. A broken heart can be almost unbearable. Proverbs 18:14 says, "The spirit of a man will sustain him in sickness, But who can bear a broken spirit?" Please don't pull back from your Heavenly Father; instead, draw near. When you pour out your pain and lay down injustice as an offering, you will feel a heavy burden lift from your shoulders. But it doesn't stop there.

Afterwards, the Lord will surround you with His presence. Psalms 91:4 (AMP) perfectly describes the preciousness of the Lord's healing love: "[Then] He will cover you with His pinions, and under His wings shall you trust and find refuge; His truth and

His faithfulness are a shield and a buckler." Come as you are and experience comfort in His presence. Let's pray. First we will deal with any difficulties in your relationship, then we will process the pain of shattered dreams.

Heavenly Father,

This is terribly painful. When I look back, I realize that there were trying times and strained conversations. Even thinking about some of these difficult moments is hard, but I don't want to carry this heaviness any longer. (Now tell the Lord about any regrets, strife, or arguments; share any tension between you or any distance in your relationship. Tell Him exactly how all of this made you feel.) Lord, this is so painful, but I bring it all to You today. Please take this ache away. I give You my hurts and I ask You to heal my heart.

Many dreams and desires also died when my dear (insert the name of your loved one) died. I did not only lose them, I lost the future that I wanted. (Now tell the Lord about any dreams or desires that were shattered when your loved one died. Tell Him how much it hurts and how you feel.) I had so many hopes, Lord, but it all fell apart around me. It hurts!

It feels so wrong; it seems so unfair. Nothing turned out how I expected. But I choose today to lay down every sense of injustice as an offering. I bring my disappointments to You and give them to You as a sacrifice. I leave them with You.

Now, Lord, I ask You to fill my heart with Your tender love, fill me with Your precious Spirit, and restore my shattered soul. I receive Your wonderful love into the depths of my heart.

In Jesus' name I pray,

Amen.

Chapter 7

CONFUSION

After I recovered from the shock of Naomi's death, the question on my lips and ringing in my mind was, "why?" Why had God, the Creator of heaven and earth, and our faithful Healer, allowed our little girl to die? His plans for us are always for good and not for evil, to give us a hope and a bright future (Jeremiah 29:11). Our Lord is a miracle-working God who can heal every disease, so why did our daughter have to pass away? This question perturbed me and I found myself coming back to the same concerns again and again. I thought that if I could just find out why she died, then I would be able to move on.

If you're confused by the pain that you're suffering, you're not alone. Many Bible heroes experienced this torment. Moses couldn't understand why he was going through so much hardship. In Numbers 11:11 (NIV), "He asked the LORD, 'Why have you brought this trouble on your servant? What have I done to displease you that you put the burden of all these people on me?'" The prophet Elijah struggled for a while to understand why a woman who showed him kindness was suffering. 1 Kings 17:20 (NLT) says, "Then Elijah cried out to the LORD, 'O LORD my God, why have you brought tragedy to this widow who has opened her home to me…'" There are many other examples of men of faith who became confused for a season in the face of suffering.

But Why?

"When I get answers, then I can start to heal!" These were my words to a friend. It just felt so unfair. We had done everything to protect our daughter throughout her short life. We prayed over her health and watched our words. We had faith for her future to be bright. At the time that Naomi died, we were serving God and His people as the pastors of our small but growing church in London. At the hospital, we prayed, praised, and believed that she would recover. After she died, we gathered a small team of prayer warriors to believe with us that she would be raised from the dead. But she never even stirred.

I don't know how your loved one died, but perhaps their suffering has led you to ask questions. "Why would a loving God allow this to happen? Where was the Lord in all this? What did we do wrong? Why me? Why us? Why that precious person?" I would see moms chain-smoke with their children by their side or watch parents curse their little ones in anger, and none of it made sense. Life often deals out difficult trials, and when it does, we can be left reeling and confused.

Getting An Answer

I sought God for help because these questions were dominating my thoughts. In my quest, I came across the testimony of a lady who had also lost her daughter. Through her story and my study, God led me to understand some vital truths. The word "why"—along with other questioning terms like who, what, when, and where—is rooted in the Hebrew word for chaos. I realized that while I was chasing an answer, it would only keep me trapped in confusion and remorse.

I then sensed the Lord ask me a question: "Could I offer you a good enough reason why your daughter had to die?" I paused before responding. "No. There is no reason that could ever be good enough for why our little girl passed away." God showed me that even if He were to tell me why, the explanation would never be sufficient for me. Then it dawned on me; I was tightly holding on to a question that had no acceptable answers. And yet that very question was trapping me in torment.

There is something else. In the book of Job, the Bible says that when God restored Job after his terrible tragedy, God gave him a double portion of everything he lost. He ended up with double the number of animals and double the amount of land. However,

Job fathered the same number of children again: ten children died during his catastrophe and he raised ten children when he was restored. Why would God double Job's animals but not double his children?

What God revealed was beautiful. When Job's children died, they simply moved to a better place. He hadn't lost any children; they were in heaven, waiting to be reunited with him in the fullness of time. God did double the size of Job's family. He had twenty sons and daughters by the time he went to be with the Lord. I realized that I needed an eternal perspective: our daughter Naomi hadn't been lost; she had changed locations.

The Turning Point

In understanding these things, I made a monumental choice. I decided to lay down the question of why. I gave up any right I felt I had to an explanation. With tears trickling down my cheeks, I knelt before the Lord. I gave up my quest for answers, and said to God, "I don't know why Naomi had to die, but I don't need to know anymore. I surrender my right to an answer. Instead, Lord, I ask You to heal my broken heart." That was one of the most important decisions in my journey to restoration.

If you had asked me before Naomi died if I could recover if I lost her, I would have told you, "No, never. She is too precious." But when I laid down my right to answers, the healing love of the Lord began to flow freely. It is all too easy for the enemy to bind our pain to our chests if we demand an explanation, because it keeps us looking backwards. When we choose a future instead of the past, God is able to lead us on a journey towards wholeness.

Kate's Battle With Regret

After Ben died at the tender age of eight, Kate was burdened by many regrets. She agonized over what she could have done better; she wished she had spent more time just holding her son and appreciating him. She felt bad for feeling so tired and overwhelmed while he was sick. Kate longed to turn back the clock and do things differently.

At our two-day conference "Healed for Life", I spoke about regret and guilt. During this session, Kate realized that she could not change the past, but now understood she could trust God for her future. This precious mom made a life-altering decision: she handed all her regrets and her "if only's" to the Lord as an offering. Almost immediately she felt a release; a heavy weight of grief lifted and a deep sadness evaporated. Kate was never again eaten up by regret.

If you have struggled with questions, holding on to the pursuit of an answer will only keep you confused. I encourage you to come to the Lord in prayer and let go. Bring your questions to God and refrain from chasing illusive answers that can never take away your pain. When you let go, you will leave your confusion behind you. Sometimes it can be helpful to ask questions, but only when you are safely out the other side of any turmoil and instead enjoying your healing.

If Only...

One type of regret that can be hard to bear is the ache of "if only". After his son was killed in battle, King David shared his terrible angst with God. 2 Samuel 18:33 says, "Then the king was deeply moved, and went up to the chamber over the gate, and wept. And as he went, he said thus: "O my son Absalom—my son, my son Absalom—if only I had died in your place! O Absalom my son, my son!"

David didn't internalize his sentiments because they were inappropriate or uncomfortable. He did not deny the depths of his emotion; he poured it all out before the Lord. God is the God of truth, so even if the cries of your heart don't seem very Christian, the Lord already knows. Keeping it buried inside will weigh you down, but when you share your thoughts and feelings with God in prayer, you will be able to lay down a heavy burden.

Maybe you can relate to the sigh of King David's heart: 'if only'. If only I had made that call. If only we had reached the hospital earlier. If only he could walk me down the isle. If only she could hold me one more time. If only I could turn back the clock. If you don't deal with the agony of 'if only', it can eat you up on the inside and leave you riddled with regret. Regret is a terribly destructive emotion. It leaves you feeling helpless, and sometimes carries with it guilt or shame.

On another occasion, King David wished he could escape from his suffering by re-winding his life: "My heart is severely pained within me...So I said 'O that I had wings like a dove! I would fly away and be at rest. Indeed, I would wander far off and remain in the wilderness. I would hasten my escape from the windy storm and the tempest.'" (Psalm 55:4-8) Denying the depth of your pain, and wishing it away, will not make it go away.

The Agony Of Regret

Let's go back to the story of Job. He suffered an unimaginable tragedy when his children died in a freak accident. As he came to terms with this horrendous calamity, he talked about his longing to be with his children again; he wished he could turn back the clock. In Job 29:2, 5b–6, he said, "Oh, that I were as in months past... When my children were around me; When my steps were bathed with cream, And the rock poured out rivers of oil for me!" He didn't push down his pain; he talked about his deep angst.

If these great men of God were taunted by remorse, please don't be surprised if the same thing happens to you. If you feel the pain of regret, don't try to sidestep the issue. Talk to the Lord from your heart. Tell Him how you feel. Give Him your angst and then please, leave it with Him.

I remember being tormented by regret after our daughter died. "Why didn't I get up in the night and go to the hospital?" I knew my little girl was very sick, but I was afraid. There I was, in the early hours of the morning, frozen by confusion and anxiety. I knew in my heart that my sweetheart needed help. However, fear bound me so I didn't get her to the hospital in time. When she needed me the most, I wasn't there for her and our precious daughter died before her second birthday. I was gripped with guilt.

The Way Out Of Regret

Probably one of the most incredible Scriptures in the Bible is God's promise that He will turn any and every situation around. Romans 8:28 (NASB) says, "And we know that God causes all things to work together for good to those who love God, to those who are called according to His purpose." It may even seem cruel to say this, but God is able to turn great loss around - if we will surrender to Him and believe that He is able.

I somehow found the courage to face my terrible regret, I talked to God about my desperate pain and released my distress in His presence. I surrendered my regrets and handed them over to God. Afterwards, I asked Him to somehow work it together for good.

I believe that the precious ministry I lead today was birthed out of the tragic loss of my daughter. The Lord received my surrender, He took me on a journey of restoration, and then He turned my river of pain into a spring of healing.

Who Caused Your Pain?

A woman in the Old Testament called Naomi suffered terribly. While living in a foreign country, both Naomi's husband and her two sons died. She lost the three people that were most precious to her. Eventually, she decided to move back to Bethlehem, bringing her daughter-in-law Ruth with her. Ruth 1:19b–21 (NLT) says, "When they came to Bethlehem, the entire town was excited by their arrival. 'Is it really Naomi?' the women asked. 'Don't call me Naomi,' she responded. 'Instead, call me Mara, for the Almighty has made life very bitter for me. I went away full, but the Lord has brought me home empty. Why call me Naomi when the Lord has caused me to suffer and the Almighty has sent such tragedy upon me?'"

Naomi believed the lie that God had caused her pain. We don't know why three members of this dear woman's family died, but we do know that the Creator of life is not the one who causes death. Naomi was full of despair as a result of her mistaken beliefs. Seeing the Lord as the reason for your sadness will lead to hopelessness. If you think that the Lord of All is against you, then there is little hope of finding a way out. If, like Naomi, you have believed that God was responsible for your grief, I want you to know that this is a cruel lie. The Lord never causes pain; He only ever seeks to take it away. In fact, it pains Him to see you grieve. Jeremiah 8:21 says, "For the hurt of the daughter of my people I am hurt…"

Far from causing your sadness, God sent His only Son, Jesus, from heaven to earth to bring you healing. Isaiah 61:1b (AMPC) says: "… He has sent me to bind up and heal the brokenhearted…" Again, we read in Psalms 147:3 (AMPC) that: "He heals the brokenhearted and binds up their wounds [curing their pains and their sorrows]." Your Heavenly Father is not the source of your sorrow; rather, He is the only One who can take it away.

No Way Out

There is another lie that can trap us in turmoil. Matthew 2:18b tells us about a woman who lost her sons: "Rachel weeping for her children, refusing to be comforted, because they are no more." Something inside this grief-stricken woman was refusing the comfort that she so desperately needed. She was pushing away help because there was nothing that anyone could do to bring her sons back from the dead. The finality of separation made her believe that she was beyond restoration.

After our daughter died, many people (both in church ministry and secular life) told us that we would never fully recover after the loss of our child. The assumption was that we would learn to live with the pain and that we would always miss our daughter. However, there is NO Bible verse that says that certain tragedies are too much for the Lord to heal. I cannot find a story that demonstrates that some emotional pain is too big for God. Jesus came from heaven to earth with a mission, and part of that mission was to minister healing to your precious heart.

Isaiah 53:5b (NLT) is clear: "He was beaten so we could be whole." When we are whole, nothing is missing. The AMPC version of Isaiah 53:5b says: "...with the stripes [that wounded] Him we are healed and made whole." Healing is relief in one area or another, whereas wholeness is when the work is finished. The dictionary definition of whole is: "complete; all elements properly belonging; not broken, damaged, or impaired in any way." You can be made whole.

It would be my honor to lead you in prayer. We will lay down any questions or regrets trapping you in torment, deal with any cruel lies that you have been believing, and open our hearts for a work of restoration. Even if you're not sure if each one applies to you, I encourage you to pray with me; there may be some questions hidden inside.

Heavenly Father,

I don't want this confusion any longer, so I choose to give up my quest for answers. I decide right now to stop asking and instead, I lay down every one of my questions at Your feet. (Now tell the Lord about the specific questions you are laying down, tell Him you don't need an answer.) I don't need to know why anymore. I give up my concerns and my demands. I give You my torment and every question as a sacrificial offering. I ask You, Lord, to clear away the chaos and confusion. I surrender.

I bring every regret and the ache of "if only" to You. (Now tell the Lord what you regret the most. Share any futile longings of your heart.) I choose today to give You my regrets and to lay down every "if only". I surrender Lord, I let go. Instead, I ask for Your perfect peace to fill my soul and surround my mind. I entrust my heart and life into Your Hands. Now, Lord, I ask that You would pour Your healing love into the depths of my heart.

Heavenly Father, I am sorry that I held You responsible in some way for my pain. I thought You were part of my problem, but I was wrong. You are a good, good Father, and You only want the best for me. I now know that my suffering was not Your doing. I don't understand why it all happened, but I know that You are not to blame. You are the only One who can help me and heal me, so I ask for Your forgiveness for blaming You. I ask You to restore my soul.

Father, I thank You that there is no loss or tragedy that You cannot heal. You are more than able to heal me and to make me whole. What You have done for others, I ask You to do for me. So today, I surrender my sadness and sorrow. I pursue the healing that You have for me. I open up to Your restoring love and I ask You to heal every broken piece of my heart.

In Jesus' name,

Amen.

Chapter 8

HELPFUL HABITS

Laughing may feel downright wrong when you are grieving, but it is actually a tonic. Science confirms through multiple studies that laughter lessens stress and soothes tension. The world-famous Mayo Clinic asserts that laughing may even ease the ache by causing your body to produce its own natural painkillers. This only confirms what Proverbs 17:22 (AMP) tells us: "A happy heart is good medicine and a cheerful mind works healing, but a broken spirit dries up the bones." Even just giggling will help lift your spirits. You may say that you don't feel like laughing; I understand. However, if a funny movie or a witty friend makes you chuckle, please don't hold back or feel bad; let yourself laugh. It is good for you.

Emotional pain can be exhausting. When you're walking through the valley of the shadow of death described in Psalm 23, you need strength. One way to build yourself up in the midst of sorrow is to pursue joy. Nehemiah 8:10 says, "...the joy of the

LORD is your strength." It may sound like a contradiction in terms, but you can experience joy in the midst of sorrow. More often than not, getting joy has to be intentional, but the strength it produces is life-giving. The fastest way I know to generate joy is to praise the Lord from your heart.

After his son died, Frank found prayer difficult because his mind would inevitably wander to his heartbreak. He usually found himself crying during soft worship so found that hard too. It was in the middle of his most painful season that Frank discovered the power of praise. He would get into the presence of God and sing at the top of his voice. Praise enabled him to take his mind off himself and fix his attention on Jesus. He often danced while he gave God glory, but the unexpected side effect was that he always felt happier and stronger afterward.

A Powerful Biblical Principle

I don't think he realized it, but Frank was practicing a Biblical principle. Jeremiah 31:13 (NLT) explains what happens when we rejoice: "The young women will dance for joy, and the men—old and young—will join in the celebration. I will turn their mourning into joy. I will comfort them and exchange their sorrow for rejoicing." After Naomi died, I praised daily. The song I sang more than any other went like this: "You have turned my mourning into dancing. You have turned my sorrow into joy!" Without even thinking about it, I was declaring the end from the beginning (see Isaiah 46:10); I was prophesying my way out of overwhelming pain.

Joy probably won't make all your pain go away, but it will strengthen you as you navigate your way through this difficult season. It might be hard to hear, but I will say it again, please pursue joy during your journey through bereavement. Ecclesiastes 3:1 says, "To everything there is a season, a time for every purpose under heaven..." It goes on to explain in verse 4 that there is: "A time to weep, and a time to laugh, a time to mourn, and a time to dance." It may at first seem insensitive, placing laughter beside weeping and dancing immediately after mourning; however, I believe they belong together as part of a healthy life.

Take Refuge In Family & Friends

After our daughter died, the utter shock made it feel as though my husband and I had been thrown out of an airplane window toward an erupting volcano below. However, we did not hit the ground. We landed on the love of our nearest and dearest. My dear friend Larissa visited the funeral director, made many of our arrangements, and even decorated our home with some precious family photographs. Other friends invited us to stay for a weekend and helped us laugh again. Some let us talk, even when we were making no sense, while still others cooked and even helped clean. The love of friends helped us through the first few weeks of life without our little one and we will be forever grateful to them for their kindness.

Ecclesiastes 4:9–12 (NLT) makes a telling statement: "Two people are better off than one, for they can help each other… If one person falls, the other can reach out and help. But someone who falls alone is in real trouble. Likewise, two people lying close together can keep each other warm. But how can one be warm alone? A person standing alone can be attacked and defeated, but two can stand back-to-back and conquer…" You will be surprised how glad people are when you ask for help. You may have to tell them what you need, but learning to look to friends and family during tough times is vital.

Galatians 6:2 (NLT) emphasizes the importance of community when we are struggling: "Share each other's burdens, and in this way obey the law of Christ." Of course, this doesn't mean we need to bear our souls with everyone, but opening up with one or two trusted friends is very helpful. Right from the start, God Himself commented on our need for one another. Genesis 2:18 reads, "And the LORD God said, 'It is not good that man should be alone; I will make him a helper comparable to him.'" Although this verse does refer to marriage, it also reveals a vital truth about our need for one another, especially during hardship. After all, Proverbs 17:17 explains, "A friend loves at all times, and a brother is born for adversity."

Keep On Keeping On

Scott Chapman, our close friend, preached at our church the Sunday after Naomi died. I can still hear some of the words of his timely message, which was entitled "Keep On Keeping On". He encouraged the precious members of our wonderful church to continue doing what they knew to do: keep praying, keep reading the word, and keep worshipping God. The enemy wants you to quit your devotionals during the storms of life; he wants you to stop fellowshipping; he wants you to retreat. However, this only makes the journey harder. I encourage you to see your healthy daily habits as the scaffolding of your life during this season.

If you usually do regular exercise, don't stop; in fact, make your fitness regime part of your therapy. I don't know how many times I have stopped in the middle of a field, halfway through a run, and cried before the Lord. He heard from heaven and restored a piece of my soul. If you like to cook or read, don't stop. Carve out time to do the things that you enjoy. You never know, you may find that you derive real pleasure from such activities earlier than you expected.

The enemy wants to keep you out of fellowship with other believers and he wants to keep you out of church. When you have been bereaved, the devil will work overtime to stop you going to Bible studies and attending Sunday services. But please get back to

Christian fellowship at the earliest opportunity. Hebrews 10:25 (NLT) says, "And let us not neglect our meeting together, as some people do, but encourage one another, especially now that the day of his return is drawing near." Watching a service online is not the same as showing up in person. When you gather, you can experience the presence of God, you can listen to the Word of God, but you will also be with other believers, who can surround you with love and encouragement.

Find Someone To Help

Helping someone else in their time of need is a healthy way to momentarily distract yourself from your pain. I'm not suggesting that you start volunteering at your local homeless shelter (unless of course the Lord leads you in that direction), but it is very helpful to stop and think who might need some support. You could pray for a friend who is struggling, then send them a word of encouragement, or do some shopping for an elderly neighbor. Taking our eyes off our own hardship and reaching out to someone else can be surprisingly restorative. Let's pray.

Heavenly Father,

I want to come out the other side of this painful season, so I ask for Your help to build habits that will help me to heal. Thank You that laughter is like medicine, so I ask You to send people to me that will help me to laugh again. Thank You that praise generates joy and joy builds strength, so I ask for Your help to praise daily.

When I need support or comfort from friends or family, help me to ask. I am not designed to cope alone, so I will not isolate myself. I decide today to meet with other Christians and show up to Sunday services. I will prioritize my devotional time in order to build myself up and I will get back to the healthy habits that were previously part of my life. Help me to live each day to the full, even through this sorrow. Lead me out the other side of this season, I pray, Oh Lord.

In Jesus' name,

Amen.

Chapter 9

YOUR HEALING JOURNEY

Your healing will probably be a journey. Sometimes, the Lord restores through a series of powerful encounters in His presence. On other occasions, as you daily bring your pain to the Lord in prayer, He will heal your heart one precious piece at a time. Your process may be lengthy or it could be quicker than you expect. Every time I have lost someone I love, the Lord has mended my broken heart, but He took me on a different journey on each occasion. Complete restoration is available to you too. Please look to the Lord every step of the way. In this chapter, I will cover certain principles that will help you to continue being healed until you are made whole.

God's Heart Toward You

The Lord treasures the moments you spend in His presence. Your Heavenly Father is never in a rush; in fact, He has all the time you need. When you talk to

Him, He is not distracted, He is not looking past you, trying to catch the eye of someone else. He is fully present and gives you His undivided attention. Sometimes we assume that God is like people, so we think He is uninterested in our difficulties, but Jeremiah 29:12 says, "Then you will call upon Me and go and pray to Me, and I will listen to you." When you talk to the Lord, He listens with a heart full of love. Psalms 34:15b (MSG) reveals God's tender attentiveness: "…His ears pick up every moan and groan."

The Lord affectionately watches over every step you take on your journey through grief. Psalms 56:8 explains: "You number my wanderings; put my tears into Your bottle; are they not in Your book?" When you cry in His presence, your tears are so dear to Him that He keeps each one in a bottle and even journals about your time together. Let's look at the same verse in the Passion: "You've kept track of all my wandering and my weeping. You've stored my many tears in your bottle—not one will be lost. For they are all recorded in your book of remembrance." (Psalms 56:8. TPT). Every one of your pained prayers is precious to the Lord.

Your Heart's Design

Your soul was made in the image of God's soul (see Genesis 1:27) for the giving and receiving of love. That's one of the reasons why losing someone you

63

love hurts so much. Your heart was made to be a vessel for fellowship; it was not designed to house pain. We must not allow grief to make our hearts its new permanent home. Allowing sadness to live in our souls is like giving strangers permission to reside in our houses. Pain doesn't belong in your heart any more than squatters belong in your home. I know how horrible grief can be, but please pursue your restoration.

To ensure our hearts can be freed from the heavy weight of pain, the Lord gave us an eviction mechanism for sorrow called crying. Tears freely released in the presence of the Lord can bring immense relief. In truth, not all weeping brings healing. Many people cry out of frustration or hurt without getting restored. However, when we learn how to surrender our sadness and pour out our hearts before the face of the Lord, we will be made whole. I have had the privilege of leading countless people to restoration. Men and women of all ages and backgrounds who have suffered terrible loss have been healed when they have released their pain in the presence of God.

I often see folk working hard to hold back. I can't tell you how many times people have apologized to me for crying while I'm ministering to them. However, the ability to weep is a device given to us by God to enable us to release our pain. Ecclesiastes 3:1 says, "To everything there is a season, a time for every purpose under heaven." A list of life's essential

purposes follows, then in verses 3 and 4 it says, "…
A time to break down… A time to weep…" If you're
reading this book, and grief is surfacing, then this is
that time. Please don't bite your lip, swallow hard,
or do anything else to try to subdue the pain. Let it
out before the Lord.

There is a big difference between a few tears and
pouring out pain. In Psalm 18:6, David said, "I cried
out to You in my distress… and… you heard my
troubled cry. My sobs came right into Your heart
and You turned Your face to rescue me." (TPT).
Crying out is not the same as crying. When we cry
out, there is a thrust behind our tears and agony
leaves. Crying is simply tears falling. After the death
of a loved one, there is usually a reservoir of pain
trapped inside. It needs to be released. David knew
how to let go in God's presence. In Psalms 6:6 (NLT),
he said, "I am worn out from sobbing. All night I
flood my bed with weeping, drenching it with my
tears." When you have suffered a great deal, you
need to pour out your pain in prayer.

Bitter Tears Or Healing Tears?

Another important point is that crying bitter tears is
not the same as surrendering your pain in God's
presence. Bitter tears are rooted in a sense of injustice,
and are usually laden with frustration. They want an
explanation. When we come into the presence of the
Lord, we must be willing to let go of our sorrow.

Lamentations 2:19b says, "...Pour out your heart like water before the face of the Lord. Lift your hands toward Him..." Lifting your hands is a universal sign of surrender. While we hold tightly to our right to be upset, we pave the way for a hard journey. When we surrender every ounce of pain in the presence of the Lord, He is able to bring lasting restoration. I encourage you to make the decision to relinquish your right to remain in pain. Letting go is not easy, but in the end, it leads to peace and genuine relief.

Adults often tell children to dry their eyes. Crying is seen by some as unnecessary emotionalism, reinforced by a popular myth that real men don't cry. This is not true; in fact, it is a lie from the enemy. Any culture that teaches that weeping is weakness is wrong. Joseph, one of the Bible's greatest leaders, sobbed in public and in private on eight separate occasions (see Genesis 42:24, 43:30, 45:2,14,15, 46:29, 50:1,17). He cried in his brother's arms and as he embraced his father. Not once did he seem ashamed or embarrassed. In fact, he cried freely and frequently—even though he was the second most powerful man in the land.

It is not only Joseph who knew how to weep. We have countless Biblical examples of mighty men pouring out their hearts, both in private and public. Jeremiah has been called the "weeping prophet" by some. King David—the man after God's own heart (see Acts 13:22)—cried frequently as he shared his pain with the Lord. Let me repeat Psalm 6:6–7 (AMP) where David wrote: "I am weary with my groaning; all night I soak my pillow with tears, I drench my couch with my weeping. My eye grows dim because of grief…" Paul the apostle cried (see Acts 20:37) and Jesus, the Lion of the tribe of Judah, wept (see John 11:35). You never need to be ashamed or embarrassed about crying; in fact, you probably need to weep frequently as you deal with your grief.

Telling The Truth—To Yourself and God

Many times, we don't know what is really going on deep down inside. Sometimes the way we feel may be uncomfortable, so our hearts tell us a different, more palatable story. Jeremiah 17:9 (AMP) says, "The heart is deceitful above all things… Who can know it [perceive, understand, be acquainted with his own heart and mind]?" We may struggle to acknowledge the true state of our relationship with our loved one before they died, so instead focus on how others let us down. We might not want to admit that we are angry with God, so we end up projecting our frustration at someone who represents Him in our lives.

Jesus is the way, the truth, and the life (see John 14:6), the Holy Spirit is called the Spirit of Truth (John 16:13) and God desires truth in our hearts (Psalm 51:6). The Lord longs to help us release our truth before Him. If you don't know why you feel stuck, ask the Holy Spirit to shine His light into your heart and reveal the reasons. Once you understand why you have been stagnant, it's time to talk to the Lord. When you tell your Heavenly Father how you really feel, you will begin to unblock your soul. Your pain may be buried underneath uncomfortable truths. Facing how you really feel will enable you to unearth blocked emotion. Telling God about any regret, guilt, anger, or feelings of injustice will allow you to offload a heavy weight in His presence. He already knows the truth; talking to Him, and then surrendering these matters, will bring relief and restoration.

Say It Like It Really Is...

After recovering in hospital, my American spiritual mother Cathy Lechner suddenly went downhill fast. I was about to leave home to minister at our Bible academy when her daughter Jerusha called me with the tragic news: "Mom's heart stopped beating a few minutes ago." It felt like someone had stabbed me in the chest. Nonetheless, I had to minister, so I gathered myself together, left the house, drove to our church and taught a roomful of eager students. I made my way through the time of ministry, then headed back home with a broken heart.

I have never met a more affirming human being. She was the greatest cheerleader anyone could wish to have. Not many ministers have a true mentor. I had the privilege of being coached and constantly encouraged by this unique lady. Every time I pictured her face, the pain intensified. Tears kept falling.

The evening she died, my son sent me a recording of his first ever preaching. As I listened to Benj share the word of God, I felt so proud of him. All of a sudden, I cried out, "I don't want to tell You, Lord! I want to tell my mama!" (I always shared my children's milestones with Prophet Cathy because she prayed daily for them both). I fell to the floor and wept. Pain from the deep recesses of my soul streamed out as I cried before the Lord. I wept hard and loud before God. I told Him exactly what was hurting me in that moment. It was a bit brutal, but it was the truth, and it released my healing. After a while, my tears dried up and I went to bed.

The Lord can handle the truth, even if it sounds irreverent. He knows the secrets of our hearts and, as David wrote in Psalms 139:1-2 (NLT), "O Lord, you have examined my heart and know everything about me. You know when I sit down or stand up. You know my thoughts even when I'm far away." God knew David's thoughts and He knows yours and mine. God knows that I love Him with my everything, but in that moment, I did not want to share with my Heavenly Father. I wanted to talk to my spiritual mother. When I cried out that night, the words I said released a ball of pain that was bound up inside.

The following morning, I didn't hurt the way I did the day before. God had started healing me. My heart still hurt, yet not as badly as before. A week later, I was in Maryland in the USA ready to run one of our Healed for Life conferences. I went for a walk early in the morning. As I worshipped, more pain surfaced so I shared my sadness with the Holy Spirit. I wept - gently this time - as I walked and talked with the Lord. This encounter was not as dramatic as the first one. However, it was just as healing. I had two other significant healing experiences in the weeks afterwards as the Lord restored me. Healing is a journey. We know when we have arrived because we don't hurt anymore. We are free.

Your Thought Life

Negative thoughts drain your energy and make painful times even more difficult. The enemy whispers lies in your ears, such as: "I can't handle this anymore", "This is too much", or "What's the point of my life?" Job 4 explains how negative thoughts creep in, often at night, influencing our feelings and our wellbeing: "Now a word was secretly brought to me, and my ear received a whisper of it. In disquieting thoughts from the visions of the night, When deep sleep falls on men, Fear came upon me, and trembling, Which made all my bones shake." (Job 4:12–13)

When you are grieving, dark thoughts can bombard your mind. Proverbs 23:7 explains that what you meditate on influences your life: "As a man thinks in his heart, so is he." In other words, we are a product of our inner thoughts. The problem can be made worse by the snowball effect. One rogue negative idea often triggers an avalanche of sorrow. Sometimes we need to listen to our thoughts and challenge anything that isn't true. For example, I won't allow myself to think thoughts like: "This is the worst" or "I can't take this anymore." Those sentiments contradict what Scripture says and will only make things feel worse. If you are struggling with thoughts like these, I believe my book, *My Pretend Friend*, will help you enormously.

It is important in this season that you practice silencing dark or negative thoughts. When despair tries to invade, turn away from those whispers and look to Jesus. The Psalmist wrote in Psalms 121:1–2 (NIV), "I lift up my eyes to the mountains— where does my help come from? My help comes from the LORD, the Maker of heaven and earth." Please don't dwell on thoughts of despair and instead remind yourself that you will come out the other side strong. Others have been where you are and have experienced the healing of the Lord; you will too.

Philippians 4:8 (NIV) says, "Finally, brothers and sisters, whatever is true, whatever is noble, whatever is right, whatever is pure, whatever is lovely, whatever is admirable—if anything is excellent or praiseworthy—think about such things." Try not to tolerate bleak thought patterns; instead, turn your mind to topics that bring you hope. Remember, this is not about pushing pain down. Give every hurt to

God in prayer, but work hard to prevent despair from taking root in your soul.

Give Yourself A Break

You probably already know that grief can be exhausting. Weeping from deep down inside can drain your energy, leaving you feeling spent. I encourage you to schedule time out, days away, or even vacations while you are journeying through bereavement. A night at the movies, a meal out with friends, or a trip to the beach might be just what you need to recharge your batteries. Sometimes it's good to set aside some time when you will not talk about your loss, but instead look to have some fun. As we learned in Chapter 8, laughter is much-needed medicine, especially during times of sorrow.

I encourage you to look at your calendar and plan some light relief. Think about the people you know who are fun to be around. Consider which activities you enjoy. My dearest friend agreed during a season of sorrow to plan fun nights out with me each month. It was therapy to my soul and always left me feeling refreshed. Let's pray.

Heavenly Father,

Thank You for Your amazing love for me and for Your desire for my complete restoration. I am so grateful that our times together mean so much to You. Lord, I ask for Your help to stay on my healing journey and to face all my pain, even sorrow that is hidden. Help me, Lord, to face the truth and to come to You every time I am hurting. (If the Lord has brought memories to you while you have been reading, tell Him all about it now. Share your deepest thoughts and feelings.)

I choose to surrender my sorrow. I loosen my grip on my grief and instead, I let go of my right to remain in pain. I don't want to live a half-life for the rest of my days, so I choose to give You my heart and my soul. I surrender to You, Oh Lord.

I don't want to tolerate dark thoughts that will make this journey even harder. I ask for Your help to recognize negativity, Lord. Please give me the strength to kick out ideas that will drag me down. I choose today to replace despair with thoughts of hope about my future because You hold my life in Your hands.

I will pursue my healing until there is no more sadness in my soul. I look to You to bring me to restoration and wholeness.

In Jesus' name,

Amen.

Chapter 10

A NEW SEASON

After our daughter died, and even after God had healed my heart, I saw myself as a bereaved mother. When I met new people, I was always aware of who knew what I had gone through, and who did not know my story. It is one thing to have a painful scar; it is another thing to see that scar as a mark that sets you apart. God's desire is that we are branded by His love, not our suffering. Song of Songs 2:4 (AMPC) says, "He brought me to the banqueting house, and his banner over me was love [for love waved as a protecting and comforting banner over my head when I was near him]." This paints a picture of God's desire for you. He wants His love to heal you deep down and to be the identifying mark over your life.

Let's look again at the Old Testament story of Naomi. Like me, this precious lady's identity had been branded by tragedy. Ruth 1:19–20 describes the day she returned home: "Now the two of them went until they came to Bethlehem. And it happened, when they had come to Bethlehem, that all the city was excited because of them; and the women said, 'Is this Naomi?' But she said to them, 'Do not call me Naomi; call me Mara…'" Naomi means "delightful", whereas Mara means "bitter". Pain and difficulty affected this woman's view of herself to such an extent that she tried to change her name. The enemy wants to muddy your self-image too.

Laying Down A Muddied Identity

Proverbs 23:7 says, "As a man thinks in his heart, so is he…" Any time our identity is rooted in pain, it will affect our thoughts and influence our decisions. Ultimately, it will guide the direction of our lives. When we go through life-shattering circumstances, it is easy for us to believe that our pain is worse than the hurts of others. Our view of our suffering sets us apart in our own hearts, but it also keeps us trapped in a season of sadness and makes it even harder to build for the future.

If I believe I have been through more suffering than others, I will also think that I am different. When we see ourselves as different, we may accept isolation and hopelessness; we could think that we cannot be restored the way others have been. We feel as though we are watching everyone else live their lives on the other side of a glass screen. All too often, it makes us feel like giving up.

One day, God ministered to me in a life-changing encounter. I sensed the Lord ask me to imagine myself picking up my dear daughter Naomi and giving her a big hug. I held her in my arms and cuddled her. Then, in my mind's eye, He asked me to place Naomi into the arms of my Heavenly Father. With tears streaming down my cheeks, I gave my little girl to Him. Afterward, I sensed the Lord ask me to surrender my identity as a victim mother. I had not realized that my inner image had been marked by tragedy, but it was true.

Just as you would remove a coat, I took off that bereaved-mom uniform and laid it down. With my garments of victimhood removed, I immediately knew who I was. Far from being a battle-weary mother, I realized that I was a dearly loved daughter of God. I was free from a heavy burden that I had no idea I was carrying.

If your loss has affected your picture of yourself, I would love to lead you in a prayer of surrender at the end of this chapter. It may feel like a painful step to take, but it will enable you to embrace the future in a healthy way. You can honor the memory of your loved one by ensuring their legacy lives on in you—I will share how later on in this chapter. That will enable you to remain connected to those who have graduated to glory through the good they did, not the pain of their departure.

Navigating New Plans

The enemy seeks to use grief to extinguish your hope. When hope fades, difficult emotions can become overwhelming because hope provides inner stability. Hebrews 6:19 says, "This hope we have as an anchor of the soul, both sure and steadfast…" That's not all, hopelessness leads to sickness of the soul. Proverbs 13:12a says, "Hope deferred makes the heart sick…" Even though it may be painful to imagine good days ahead, it is vital for your wellbeing. Looking forward to something good on the horizon will help you heal.

One of the Bible's best-loved verses reveals a precious truth. Jeremiah 29:11 (ESV) says, "For I know the plans I have for you, declares the LORD, plans for welfare and not for evil, to give you a future and a hope." Notice that this Scripture speaks about plans in the plural. God does not have just one plan for you; He has many. When your life takes a heartbreaking detour, your Heavenly Father is able to reroute your course. Your picture of the future may have been shattered, but I want you to know that the Lord can still create a life for you that is filled with joy. It may take time to get back up and find the strength to dream again, but Jesus is your Master Restorer. I encourage you to think about opportunities in your future and make plans that will stir hope in your heart. It will shorten your journey out of the wilderness.

The Void

When you lose someone you love, it's not just the grief that hurts; their departure often leaves a void in your life. It's that empty space that often causes people to miss someone for years, and even decades, after they pass away. The Lord taught me a precious principle that can lift such a weight. With the exception of physical affection, the Lord really can meet all our needs. John 15:4a (AMP) says, "Dwell in Me, and I will dwell in you. [Live in Me, and I will live in you.]" He is able to fill even the biggest of shoes.

After my spiritual mother passed away, any time I missed her friendship or wise counsel, I looked to the Lord and asked Him to occupy that empty space. I asked Him to reveal Himself to me as my mentor and nurturing friend. Any time I felt a longing to be with her, I got into God's presence and asked Him to heal my heart and draw close to me. I looked to the Lord to fill the void that her untimely death left in my heart and life. Gradually, I felt Him fill the empty places that her death left behind. Her absence ended up creating a new closeness with the Lord.

Psalms 4:8 says, "I will both lie down in peace, and sleep; for You alone, O LORD, make me dwell in safety." The Hebrew word for peace is shalom, which means "well, happy, friendly, healthy, prosperous, and at peace". It also means "nothing missing", "nothing broken". Any time you are missing your loved one, ask the Lord to pour His love into your heart; He is able to fill every empty space.

Honoring Their Memory

Less than a year after our daughter died, we were blessed with a son. During the first few weeks of Benjy's life, I struggled with some uncomfortable emotions. Every time I told my sweet baby boy that I loved him, I felt pangs of guilt, as though I was somehow betraying Naomi. Of course, I knew these feelings were irrational, but they would not go away. The way I dealt with these thorny feelings was to affirm that I still loved Naomi any time I expressed my love for Benjy, but I knew that that was not the answer.

My daughter and I used to love singing a particular worship song together. I would hold Naomi in my arms and spin around as we sang, "He has turned my mourning into dancing…" After she died, I often lifted this song of praise to the Lord in my secret place. It became a very significant chorus that signified my journey. One Sunday morning during worship, as I held my son in my arms, our band began to lead us in that song. At first I froze; uncomfortable thoughts and feelings bombarded my soul, but I made a decision to give God a very special sacrifice of praise. With Benjy in my arms, I lifted up my voice to the Lord and spun around at the word "turn". In that moment, all guilt lifted and joy filled my heart, then I heard the Lord speak to me: "Naomi taught you how to love. Through Benjy, your 'mother heart' will grow bigger."

The Legacy Of Your Loved One

Those words set me free and I learned a valuable lesson. When someone you love passes away, they leave a legacy, a mark for good on your life. Naomi taught me how to be a mother. Your loved one may have imparted wisdom, they could have showed you valuable skills, they might have demonstrated love, or modeled a life of gratitude. Paul the apostle rejoiced when he saw the faith of Timothy's relatives living on in him. 2 Timothy 1:5 (NLT) says, "I remember your genuine faith, for you share the faith that first filled your grandmother Lois and your mother, Eunice. And I know that same faith continues strong in you." Timothy's grandmother left a legacy that lived on in him long after she graduated to glory.

My American spiritual mother was one of the most tender-hearted human beings I have ever met. She had time for people, even when she was exhausted. Her face shone with kindness as she smiled at each person that she passed as she walked to the front of a church to minister. After she died, I coined a phrase: "Let her legacy of love live on in me." Identifying the legacy that your loved one has left behind will help you to pick up any baton they left behind and embrace the future with purpose. Even if your relationship was strained, you will be able to find something good that they gave you, even if that is simply your life. Let's pray.

Heavenly Father,

I ask for Your help to come out the other side of this grief. I don't want pain to brand my life, so today I choose to give You any aspect of my identity that has been marked by loss. (Now tell the Lord how your experiences have affected your view of yourself. Acknowledge any way that bereavement has impacted your inner image. If you have seen yourself as a victim, tell the Lord now.) I lay down any aspect of my identity that has been branded by tragedy. I lay it at Your feet, Lord Jesus. I remove the cloak of victimhood off my shoulders and I give it to You. Thank You, Lord, that I am marked by Your great love, thank You that my identity comes from being Your well-loved child.

Many dreams were shattered when (insert the name of your loved one) died. (Now tell the Lord about any particular dreams that come to mind. Share your sorrow and the pain you feel about those hopes being devastated.) Thank You that You still have good plans for me, thank You that You still have a future for me. I ask for Your help to see the light at the end of this tunnel and to embrace the opportunities that lie ahead.

I miss (insert the name of your loved one); they left an empty place in my heart and life. I ask You, Lord, to fill the void they left behind. Reveal Yourself to me in new ways and I ask You to draw close any time I feel their absence. I am grateful for what I learned or received through (insert the name of your loved one). I choose today to allow their legacy to live on in me.

I embrace the future, knowing that You are by my side. Every time I am hurting, I will come to You and ask You to heal my heart. I will stay on my healing journey until my soul is fully restored. Thank You that I will be made whole again. Thank You that there is joy in my future. Thank You that You still have good plans for my life.

In Jesus' name I pray,

Amen.

WHAT NEXT?

Your heart is no doubt your most valuable, and yet your most vulnerable, asset. This book is just part of your journey to healing and freedom. As you finish this book, make the decision to continue to prioritize your inner wellbeing. Visit JoNaughton.com to find out about our resources to help you to wholeness. The Heart Academy provides life-changing courses by Zoom including: "Life After The Death Of A Loved One", but also on other topics, such as "Breaking The Power Of Rejection", "Unblocking Your Emotions", and "Overcoming Insecurity". We have a mentoring network, online courses, and a range of print, digital, and audiobooks. We run half-day, full-day, and two-day events, all designed to help you and your family on your journey.

"I am convinced and sure of this very thing, that He who began a good work in you will continue until the day of Jesus Christ (right up to the time of His return), developing [that good work] and perfecting and bringing it to full completion in you." (Philippians 1:6, AMP) Let that word sink deep into you. God is at work in your heart and life. He has already started the job, and He will be faithful to finish it.

A SPECIAL INVITATION

If you would like to ask Jesus to become the Lord of your life, I would be honored to lead you in a simple prayer. The Bible says that God loves you and that Jesus wants to draw close to you: "Behold I stand at the door and knock. If anyone hears My voice and opens the door, I will come in." (Revelation 3:20) If you would like to know Jesus as your Friend, your Savior, and your Lord, the first step is to ask. Pray this prayer:

Dear Lord,

I know that You love me and have a wonderful plan for my life. I ask You to come into my heart today and be my Savior and Lord. Forgive me for all my sins, I pray. Thank You that because You died on the cross for me, I am forgiven of every wrong I have ever committed when I repent. I give my life to You entirely and ask You to lead me in Your ways from now on.

In Jesus' name,

Amen.

If you have prayed this prayer for the first time, it will be important to tell a Christian friend what you prayed and to find a good church. Just as a newborn baby needs nourishment and care, so you (and all Christians) need the support of other believers as you start your new life as a follower of Jesus Christ.

You can watch free Bible messages that will help to build your faith by subscribing to my YouTube channel and to Harvest Church London's YouTube channel. You can follow me on Instagram (@naughtonjo), go on Facebook and like my public page (Jo Naughton), and follow me on X (@naughtonjo). God bless you!

ABOUT THE AUTHOR

Jo Naughton is the founder of Whole Heart Ministries, which is dedicated to helping people be free to fulfill their God-given purpose. Together with her husband, Paul, Jo pastors Harvest Church in London, England. A public relations executive turned pastor, Jo's previous career included working for King Charles (while he was Prince) as an Executive VP of his largest charity. After reaching the pinnacle of the public relations world, Jo felt the call of God to full-time ministry. She is a regular guest on TV and radio shows in the US and UK.

An international speaker and author, Jo ministers with a heart-piercing anointing, sharing with great personal honesty in conferences and at churches around the world. Her passion is to see people set free from all inner hindrances so that they can fulfill their God-given destiny. Countless people have testified to having received powerful and life-changing healing through her ministry. Jo and Paul have two wonderful children, Ben and Abby.

You can connect with Jo via:

JoNaughton.com

Instagram (@naughtonjo)

YouTube (Jo Naughton)

Facebook (public page – Jo Naughton)

For more information about Harvest Church London, visit harvestchurch.org.uk

ALSO BY THE AUTHOR:

INSERT FRONT COVER IMAGES of *Lifting the Mask, Dreamstealers, 30-Day Detox for your Soul, Doorway to your Destiny, My Whole Heart, The Many Faces of Shame, My Pretend Friend, Let's Talk About Trauma, Destiny Blockers, How To Rise from The Ashes of Tragedy, My Heart Matters, Parents Please Read, How to Survive the ABC's of Life & Leadership.*

All of Jo Naughton's books are available at: JoNaughton.com

www.ingramcontent.com/pod-product-compliance
Lightning Source LLC
Chambersburg PA
CBHW030959090426
42737CB00007B/607